God-Centred Priorities

Five Principles For Making Wise Decisions

Ray Trainer

British Library Cataloguing in Publication Data
A record for this book is available from the British Library

ISBN: 978-1-84625-698-1

Cover design by Kathryn Chedzoy

Printed in the UK

DayOne, Ryelands Road, Leominster, HR6 8NZ
Email: sales@dayone.co.uk
Website: www.DayOne.co.uk

Contents

To the senior youth group at Hoylake Evangelical Church to whom I taught these principles on guidance.

I am thankful to my immediate family, Don Crisp, Lawrie Gartside, Helen Gray, Trevor Jones, Rachel Lindsay, and Sue Trainer for their advice and encouragement. I am also thankful to Judy Trainer for the illustration.

Introduction

There's an often-recounted story, which is probably not true, of a young, recently-converted Christian who woke up one morning feeling somewhat listless. As a typical teenager, he wasn't quite sure what to do with himself that day. However, though young in the faith, he did know that the Bible was important, for he had been correctly taught that it was sufficient in all matters of faith and practice. So this young Christian decided to turn to his Bible to help him choose what to do. He picked it up, flicked randomly through its pages, and found himself reading Matthew 27:5: 'So Judas threw the money into the temple and left. Then he went away and hanged himself.' That didn't sound very promising, so he decided to give it another go. Again he flicked through its pages and picked a verse at random. This time it was Luke 10:37: 'Jesus told him: "Go and do likewise."'

Of course, we may smile at the innocence of that young Christian, but often we also make decisions based upon incorrect grounds, for decision making is rarely a matter of dutifully adhering to a simple and straightforward set of rules. In other words, if we just follow the right procedure – A, B, and then C – then we can't go far wrong, can we? In addition, specifically for the big issues of life, making good choices is never easy. Whom do I marry? Where do I live? What employment shall I pursue? These are major decisions which all require much thought and should not be hastily rushed into. However, too often the reality is that we do make such decisions with little thought or, more likely, based upon unwise principles.

So what should we do? What can we turn to that will help us make wise decisions? What can we rely on as a reliable guide for correct living? The answer, of course, is the Bible, although there is, as we observed with that young, recently-converted Christian, a wrong way to use it. Nevertheless, the Bible is God's pre-eminent instructions for us so that we might make wise and godly choices and so live as he would have us live. Psalm 119:105 reveals this truth to us: 'Your word is a lamp to my feet, a light on my path,' as does 2 Timothy 3:16: 'All

Scripture is God-breathed and useful for teaching, rebuking, correcting and training in righteousness, so that the servant of God may be thoroughly equipped for every good work.'

In particular, one way the Bible guides us is to give specific moral commands for us to obey. The example which comes immediately to mind is the Ten Commandments found in Exodus 20:1–17 and Deuteronomy 5:6–21, though there are many other examples I could point to. Of course, the Bible does not have a precise rule for every situation we face in life. Clearly, that would be impossible. In addition, situations change and rules laid down for those living when the Bible was written may not actually be so relevant to our own very-different, modern-day world. As a result, the Bible gives us principles as well. Though these principles may not be as easy to understand as simple, precise rules, it's these principles which we have to be aware of and follow in our everyday lives. An example of such a principle, concerning the practical support of gospel workers, is seen, explained and applied by Paul, in 1 Corinthians 9:7–14 and 1 Timothy 5:17–18. In other words, in order to know what we should do from the Bible, we need constantly to understand and apply the principles on guidance which God in the Bible has graciously provided for us.

Yet, it's worth asking why this is important? Why not simply drift through life casually making decisions with little or no forethought? The straightforward answer is that all people are accountable to God for everything they do and this includes the decisions they make. Yes, as we know, Christians are free in Jesus Christ, as Galatians 5:1 explains: 'It is for freedom that Christ has set us free. Stand firm, then, and do not let yourselves be burdened again by a yoke of slavery.' But this freedom must be used wisely in order to serve each other, Galatians 5:13: 'But do not use your freedom to indulge the flesh; rather, serve one another humbly in love.' Therefore, understanding and applying biblical principles on guidance is important because we're accountable to God for all that we say, think, and do.

Yet there's a further reason for why we need to take time over these things, for consider Psalm 90:12. Moses prays: 'Teach us to number our days, that we may gain a heart of wisdom.' In other words, Moses is seeking perspective from God on life within this world, that our lives are but temporary and this present-day world will one day pass away, whereas, as Moses informs us back in Psalm 90:2, God is 'from everlasting to everlasting'. God has always been and will always be and, in comparison, our own momentary lives are just like a fleeting mist on a fresh summer morning.

Notice also that Moses seeks this perspective on life – where we are, where we're headed, what's important – so that he might live wisely. In effect, he's asking God to help him have God-centred priorities. At the beginning of the twentieth-century, pioneer missionary Henry Morrison

10

returned home to New York after faithfully serving the Lord in Africa for forty years. On the boat which brought Henry Morrison home was the wildly popular President Theodore Roosevelt. Indeed, as the boat entered New York Harbour, Roosevelt was greeted with a joyous fanfare. Henry Morrison felt somewhat dejected; after all, he'd spent a long time in Africa in the Lord's service. Then a thought came to Henry Morrison, 'Henry, you're not home yet.' His perspective on life – at least, after that moment's thought – was right, for like Moses he sought to understand the brevity of life and the impact of that much-needed truth on what's important. We must do the same, for we also need 'to number our days'. We also require principles on guidance, as revealed in the Bible, to make perceptive choices based upon good priorities.

This is what this book is all about. We will consider five important biblical principles on how to make wise decisions. One is the foundation, three are pillars resting on the foundation, and the fifth is the all-embracing arch supported by those underlying pillars. My initial understanding of these five principles took shape while I was studying Philippians 1 in preparation for a series of sermons. In Philippians 1:10 Paul prays that the Christians in Philippi 'may be able to discern what is best'. In Philippians 1:12–26 Paul answers this prayer, in part, by revealing his own priorities in life. Some years later I read True Spirituality by Vaughan Roberts.[1] In 1 Corinthians 8–10, Paul applies the same priorities found in Philippians 1 to answer a thorny question asked of him by the Corinthian church, a question, as we see in 1 Corinthians 8:1, 'about food sacrificed to idols'. In confirmation of my own understanding from Philippians 1, Vaughan Roberts clearly and carefully explains, in his book, these same priorities or principles on guidance.

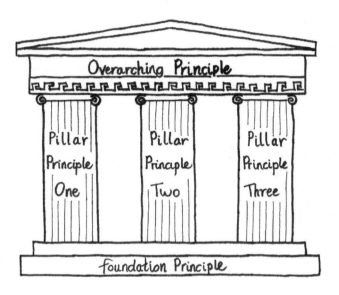

This booklet encompasses material used in sermon series on Romans, 1 Corinthians, and Philippians and also teaching on guidance given to the senior youth group of my local church. My aim is that it will be of benefit to those who read it so that we make wise decisions for God's glory.

What we shouldn't rely on

I remember, as a young Christian, being taught about guidance. Two assertions in particular come to mind. First, I was told that God's will consists of three aspects. There's the sovereign aspect, which is God's secret purpose for everything that happens within this world. In Daniel 4:35 King Nebuchadnezzar states: 'He [the Most High] does as he pleases with the powers of heaven and the peoples of earth. No one can hold back his hand or say to him: "What have you done?"' In Acts 2:23 Peter declares: 'This man [Jesus of Nazareth] was handed over to you by God's deliberate plan and foreknowledge; and you, with the help of wicked men, put him to death by nailing him to the cross.' There's also the moral aspect, which is God's revealed instructions for how we should live. In Micah 6:8 the prophet says: 'And what does the LORD require of you? To act justly and to love mercy and to walk humbly with your God.' In 1 Thessalonians 4:3 Paul writes: 'It is God's will that you should be sanctified.' Finally, there's the individual aspect, which is God's all-inclusive life-plan uniquely fashioned for each person. I was further taught that discovering this individual will of God for my life was essential for me to make wise and godly decisions. Of course, the first two aspects are correct, but is the third? We will consider this further when we look at the foundational principle on guidance.

Second, I was taught a method of guidance which is based upon the illustration of a pilot's docking procedure at a certain harbour within the Mediterranean. This harbour can only be reached by sailing through a narrow channel between hazardous rocks. As a result, many ships have been lost over the years. To counter

'We have three lights to guide us: God's word, wise counsel, circumstances.'

this and to guide ships safely into port, three lights have been mounted on poles. When the lights are lined up and seen as one, then the pilot knows that he can safely bring the ship through the channel into harbour. However, if the pilot sees two or three lights, then he knows that he's in danger. Similarly, we too have three lights to guide us: God's word, wise counsel, and circumstances. In other words, if God's word allows it, the advice of others affirms it, and circumstances support it, then go ahead and do it! Now there's much that's helpful in this, but is following this somewhat simplistic formula all that's required for guidance on what to do? Can we merely rely on this set of rules or do we need – on occasion, at least – to think matters through much more carefully? To answer this, let me first of all give you six ways for guidance which should never be solely relied on.[2]

The first way is the promise box. A promise box contains Scripture verses on rolled-up pieces of paper. A verse from the box is chosen at random and then taken as the promise for that day. However, this practice doesn't actually make us more godly and wise. Indeed, doctors, lawyers, and teachers don't pass their examinations and gain their qualifications by randomly picking sentences from their textbooks! So we also shouldn't use the Bible in this undemanding way.

The second way is to continuously seek wise counsel until we hear what we want to hear. This is exemplified by an old Scottish woman who went from home to home across the countryside selling thread, buttons, and shoelaces. When she came to an unmarked crossroad, she would toss a stick into the air and go in the direction that the stick pointed to when it landed. One day, however, she was seen tossing the stick several times. 'Why do you toss the stick more than once?'

someone asked her. 'Because,' replied the woman, 'it keeps pointing to the left and I want to take the road on the right.' Many Christians are like that. They keep on asking different people for advice until they hear what they want to hear. Of course, it's not that we shouldn't seek advice, for wise counsel can be very helpful, but we mustn't do the rounds until we hear what we want to hear. In effect, such 'wise counsel' is not wise at all.

The third way is circumstances: if this happens, then I'll do that. The result is our decisions are based merely upon how our circumstances work out. Of course, some may argue that this method is biblical and point to the example of Gideon's fleece in Judges 6. This method sounds super-spiritual, for it seems to acknowledge God's sovereignty, but it isn't. Moreover, even if the decisions reached are good decisions, solely looking to circumstances is not the right way to make them, for God has given us minds to use. Therefore, this is just a lazy method which looks for shortcuts and easy options. J. I. Packer put it like this: 'If we want God to guide us ... we must be willing to think ... God made us thinking beings, and he guides our minds as we think things out in his presence.'[3] Circumstances by themselves are not enough.

The fourth way is to do nothing. In other words, we just need to pray and wait on the Lord. Of course, this also sounds super-spiritual, but again it isn't. Yes, as an aeroplane waits for the pilot to get into the cockpit before it flies, so we are to wait on the Lord. But an aeroplane still needs to get ready to fly, for it won't go far if it has no fuel in the tank and the chocks are still under its wheels. So if you need a job, send out application forms. If you need a house to live in, visit estate agents. Doing nothing is not enough.

The fifth way is dreams and visions. This is demonstrated in Acts 16:9–10: 'During the night Paul had a vision of a man of Macedonia standing and begging him, "Come over to Macedonia and help us." After Paul had seen the vision, we got ready at once to leave for Macedonia, concluding that God had called us to preach the gospel to them.' Of course, God has a right to use this method. There's no question about that. This method was also important during the infancy of the church when the Scriptures were not yet completed. Indeed, in the New Testament we see that this method is used less frequently over time and only one vision is mentioned within all the New Testament letters. The reason is that this method is inherently unreliable and therefore dangerous, for interpretation is risky: was that dream I had last night guidance from the Lord or the result of a mature piece of cheddar eaten the evening before? Even more, this method is easy to counterfeit and, as a consequence, it can lead people astray. Dreams and visions are unreliable.

The sixth way is feelings. This is guidance based upon hunches and impressions. For example, some will say that they know what to do because they have a sense of peace about it. Others will say that they have a deep conviction within. Indeed, Paul advises us in Galatians 5:25 to 'keep in step with the Spirit', so isn't this method of looking to inner feelings actually allowing the Holy Spirit to speak to us and guide us? Clearly, God does use such subjective impressions to direct us. He does lay convictions upon our hearts. However, the danger is, if this is all that we have to base our decisions upon, then this is nothing but subjectivism. We need more than that, for how do we know where those feelings come from? Does that sense of peace or deep conviction come from God or from my own sinful nature? In other words, inner feelings can be wrong. Yes, God does use impressions and feelings. He may give us a sense of peace or a deep conviction within. However, such things should be low down on the list of things we rely on to help us to make wise decisions. Feelings by themselves are not enough.

So let me summarise like this the common feature found within all these incorrect ways for guidance: they seek to short-circuit our own responsibility to carefully apply the God-given principles of the Bible for making right choices. Yes, those biblical principles may often be difficult to work through in practice, but that is our responsibility and what we have to do.

The foundational principle: do what is right

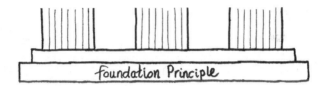

foundation Principle

A nun was going from door to door in Paris collecting money to aid the poor within the city. She came to the home of a rich free-thinker who said that he would give her a thousand francs if she would only drink a glass of champagne with him. The nun was teetotal by conviction and so struggled with her conscience and hesitated on what to do. However, after a few moment's thought and as a thousand francs meant many loaves of bread, she agreed to the request. A servant brought the bottle and poured. The nun emptied the glass in one go. Then she said, 'And now, sir, another glass, please, at the same price.' She got it!

Of course, this story is not meant to be a comment on the rights or wrongs of drinking alcohol; rather, it's to illustrate whether it's ever acceptable for us to go against our own understanding of right and wrong, as this pragmatic nun clearly did. Indeed, the answer to this is our foundational principle: we're always to do what is right and never to do what is wrong. As Philippians 1:27 helpfully points out: 'Whatever happens, conduct yourselves in a manner worthy of the gospel of Christ.' And again in Ephesians 4:22–24: 'You were taught ... to put off your old self, which is being corrupted by its deceitful desires; to be made new in the attitude of your minds; and to put on the new self, created to be like God in true righteousness and holiness.'

God has given us his moral law, which is a reflection of his own perfect character. We have the Ten Commandments. We have the ethical teaching of the Bible from Genesis through to Revelation. We're to love the Lord our God with all our heart, mind, soul, and strength. We're to love our neighbours – everyone we meet within this world – as ourselves. Therefore, as God's moral law is an expression of his own holiness, love, justice, faithfulness, and wisdom, so it should always constrain our decisions. It should shape and override everything that we decide to do. This is God's will for us: to walk blamelessly before him by obeying all his moral law.

However, as Christians, it's not so much the moral law of God which actually empowers us to do this; rather, it's the gospel, the Spirit of God, and our own day-by-day faith in Jesus Christ as these three things work harmoniously together. Indeed, the gospel encourages purity within us by reminding us of the truth of our identity in Jesus Christ. For example, as heirs of the world (Romans 4:13), why should we envy? As God's treasured possession (1 Peter 2:9), why should we be jealous? As children of the Father (Matthew 6:26), why should we be afraid? In addition, the Spirit himself reveals to us the truth of the gospel. 1 Corinthians 2:12: 'What we have received is not the spirit of the world, but the Spirit who is from God, so that we may understand what God has freely given us.' He also shows us where we need to change. 1 Thessalonians 1:5: 'our gospel came to you ... with power, with the Holy Spirit and deep conviction.' He also glorifies the Son so that our desire is to love and serve him more fully. John 16:14: 'He [the Spirit of truth] will glorify me [Jesus] because it is from me that he will receive what he will make known to you.' Our day-by-day faith in Jesus Christ also enables us to live as we ought to live. For we trust that God knows best. We trust that he loves us and cares for us. We trust that he is with us and will help us to persevere. Galatians 2:20: 'I have been crucified with Christ and I no longer live, but Christ lives in me. The life I now live I live in the body, I live by faith in the Son of God, who loved me and gave himself for me.'

Furthermore, in Colossians 1:9 Paul writes: 'For this reason, since the day we heard about you, we have not stopped praying for you. We continually ask God to fill you with the knowledge of his will through – or perhaps better translated – which consists of all the wisdom and understanding that the Spirit gives.'[4] In short, knowing God's will means having a wise understanding of how God desires us to behave and react within our fallen, fractured world. Specifically, God's will is for us to be like his Son, Jesus Christ. Romans 8:29: 'For those

'God's will is for us to be like his Son, Jesus Christ.'

God foreknew he also predestined to be conformed to the image of his Son, that he might be the firstborn among many brothers and sisters.' So which job should you get? The job that helps you to live as Jesus Christ would have you live. However, even if you make an unwise decision, you are still to live as Jesus Christ would have you live. Whom should you marry? Someone who will help you in your walk before the Lord. However, even if you make an unwise choice, you are still to walk in righteousness and holiness before God. Where should you live? The place where you can best serve the Lord and be of benefit to others, particularly to other Christians. However, even if you live a million miles away from other Christians, you are still to conduct yourself in a manner worthy of the gospel of Jesus Christ. This is God's will for you.

In effect, the picture is that we're like sheep in a field that's surrounded and protected by the fence of God's moral law. Yes, we're actually free to go wherever we want within that field, but we mustn't ever go beyond the protecting-fence of God's moral law. Now, holding that picture in mind, go back to those three aspects of God's will which I was taught as a young Christian: God's sovereign, moral, and individual will. How does the truth of this foundational, non-negotiable principle bear upon this understanding of God's will, particularly the third aspect of God's all-inclusive life-plan uniquely fashioned for each person? It doesn't fit, does it? For we can truly go freely anywhere within that field and still be within the orbit of God's will for us.

Luke, in Acts 15:28, tells us that 'it seemed good to the Holy Spirit and to us [the apostles and elders] not to burden you [the early Christians] with anything beyond the following requirements ...' The underlying Greek word translated 'it seemed good' is also found in Acts 15:22, 25. Clearly, the decision of the Jerusalem Council, which Luke is recording for us in Acts 15, involves prior thinking, debate, and the application of Scripture. So they come to a consensus. It seemed good to them. In other words, it doesn't involve the apostles and elders somehow discovering God's individual will for them. Paul, in 1 Thessalonians 3:1, tells the Thessalonian church that 'we thought it best to be left by ourselves in Athens'. Again it's clear that Paul is not attempting to discover God's individual will for his life; rather,

> 'Paul exercises his freedom of choice within the orbit of God's will.'

he's exercising his own freedom of choice within the orbit of God's moral will: he did what he thought best. To quote Friesen and Maxon: 'In non-moral decisions, the goal of the believer is to make wise decisions on the basis of spiritual expediency.'[5]

To summarise, the foundational principle is: we're always to do what is right and never to do what is wrong. As a consequence, if the Bible does not lay upon us a command to obey or a principle to follow, then we're free to choose – wisely, of course – our own direction in life, knowing that any decision which we make within the moral will of God is acceptable to God.[6] This principle could also be described as the constraint of God's moral law.

The first pillar:
love takes precedence over knowledge

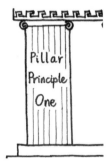

Though we have established the foundational principle on guidance – do what is right, never do what is wrong – yet there are still many decisions we have to make which are not determined by clearly-defined right and wrong. In fact, we face many thousands of such decisions each day, don't we? Some are trivial. What socks do I put on? What breakfast do I eat? Others are more serious. Whom do I marry? What job will I do? Where shall I live? Which church do I attend? So what do we need to make such decisions? We need wisdom and understanding. We need to make our decisions based upon what's important and vital. We need to have wise,

God-centred, biblical priorities. So let's consider the first of those priorities.

I recall being told about a certain Christian once observing about a controversial issue within his local church – as if this was a self-evident, unarguable axiom – 'Feelings don't matter; it's facts that count!' However, is that right? Not according to Paul in Romans 14:19, 1 Corinthians 8, and Philippians 1:21–26. First, consider Romans 14:19: 'Let us therefore make every effort to do what leads to peace and to mutual edification.' In Romans 14:1 – 15:13 Paul desires the relationship between Christians in Rome to be gospel-centred. He longs for unity. In particular, Paul is speaking to two groups of people within the churches of Rome. There are the weak and the strong. The weak considered themselves obligated to keep the Jewish food laws and to celebrate certain special days within the Jewish calendar. Effectively, they didn't appreciate the freedom they had in Jesus Christ. Of course, the weak wouldn't have referred to themselves as 'the weak'. They would probably have thought of themselves as 'the strong' because they were maintaining God's law as they saw it. In contrast, the strong knew and appreciated their freedom in Jesus Christ. They had a correct understanding of the gospel. The facts were on their side.

However, this difference between the weak and the strong was damaging the unity of the church, for the weak were condemning the strong for their lax morals and the strong were looking down their collective noses on the weak as those having an inferior understanding of the gospel. We see this in Romans 14:3. However, neither were right to think of their fellow Christians in these disparaging ways. Romans 14:4: 'Who are you to judge someone else's servant? To their own master, servants stand or fall. And they will stand, for the Lord is able to make them stand.' So how, then, are the weak and the strong to behave towards one another? The answer is found in Romans 14:19. They're to love and maintain fellowship with each other whatever it takes! Now this may sound quite shocking, but within the bounds of the gospel, united fellowship is actually more important than correct practice, for the weak were theologically wrong, yet it's the strong who have to set aside their own freedom for the sake of their weaker brothers and sisters in the Lord!

Second, consider 1 Corinthians 8. The situation in Corinth is similar to the situation in Rome. Again there are the weak and the strong. Indeed, the issue dividing the Corinthian believers is whether Christians are free to eat, at home or in the temple, food sacrificed to idols. Of course, this is something which doesn't come into our own everyday experience as Christians today, but, in a way, this is helpful, for it means that we can see the principles at work in what Paul writes without ourselves getting embroiled in the emotion of the details.

In Paul's day, animal sacrifices were a regular part of pagan worship. In practice, this meant that the pagan temple was not only a place of worship, but also the local butcher's shop and the local restaurant too. Therefore, when people went to the market to buy meat, they bought meat from the local temple which had previously been sacrificed to idols and when they went out with their friends to celebrate a big event, they went to the local temple to share a meal with them. Now this, for some believers, was a big problem.

In 1 Corinthians 8 Paul confronts this problem by looking at it from two angles. First he looks at it from the angle of knowledge and then he looks at it from the angle of love. What does he say? That love takes precedence over knowledge! 1 Corinthians 8:1–3: 'But knowledge puffs up while love builds up. Those who think they know something do not yet know as they ought to know. But whoever loves God is known by God.'

In other words, knowledge without love leads to pride and arrogance. It's like an inflated balloon with no substance within it. However, love is very different. Love desires the good of others. It's prepared to go without for the sake of others. It's not interested in rights; it's only interested in responsibilities. Indeed, love even takes risks in the knowledge and enjoyment of God's love for us. It's like the trapeze artist, performing his amazing tricks, risking life and limb; but, no, for we look below and there's the safety net. He's been safe all the time. And like that trapeze artist, we too can go out on a limb for God and his people knowing that whatever happens we remain secure in his love. Deuteronomy 33:27: 'The eternal

God is your refuge, and underneath are the everlasting arms.'

In Mark 7:19, on the occasion when Jesus tells us that 'nothing that enters a person from the outside can defile them', we're told: 'In saying this Jesus declared all foods clean.' So we can eat halal meat, black pudding, fish on Fridays, and chocolate during Lent with a clear conscience. In 1 Corinthians 8:8 Paul affirms this same truth: 'But food does not bring us near to God; we are no worse if we do not eat, and no better if we do.' So eating meat, whether or not it has been previously sacrificed to idols, makes no difference to us. We can eat it freely. And that's precisely what all Christians should know! So Paul agrees with those who're asserting their freedom and he disagrees with those who're more cautious.

Even so, love takes priority. Therefore, though our own theological understanding may rightly instruct us that we're free to do such and such within our lives, that does not necessarily mean that we should go ahead and do it, for we have to put the weaker Christian first, even if it costs us the opportunity to enjoy our own freedom. 1 Corinthians 8:13: 'Therefore, if what I eat causes my brother or sister to fall into sin, I will never eat meat again, so that I will not cause them to fall.'

Third, consider Philippians 1:21–26. Notice two small words found within verse 24: 'but it is more necessary for you that I remain in the body.' Those two words are 'for you'. Now, in the previous two verses, Paul has been wrestling with whether it's better for him to die and be with Christ or to remain alive so that he can continue to work for the benefit of the local church in Philippi. Paul is 'torn between the two', for what Paul would personally prefer is 'to depart and be with Christ, which is better by far'. Therefore, left to his own inclination, there would be no other choice for Paul. However, Paul is not interested in what's best for himself; rather, he's more concerned about what happens to the church. So he writes: 'it is more necessary for you that I remain in the body.' Paul's priority is the local church.

Putting this all together, we arrive at the second principle, which is the first pillar that rests on the foundational principle: love takes precedence over knowledge. It specifically relates to our relationship with our brothers and sisters in Jesus Christ. Moreover, we've just seen how Paul applies this principle to life within the local church of his day. So how are we to apply this principle to our own lives within our own churches today? One way, before we make any important decisions, is to ask ourselves the question: does what I plan to do cause other Christians to stumble and fall? For what matters is not what I'm free to do, but what is of benefit to my brothers and sisters in Jesus Christ. So this principle could also be described as the priority of the local church's spiritual growth and well-being. Philippians 1:25: 'Convinced of this, I know that I will remain, and will continue with all of you for your progress and joy in the faith.'

The second pillar:
the gospel takes precedence
over my rights

Pillar
Principle
Two

On 4 July 1776 the American Declaration of Independence
was adopted by the so-called Continental Congress. This
Declaration stated that the thirteen American colonies of
that day, then at war with Great Britain, now considered
themselves to be independent states and that they were
no longer part of the British Empire. Thomas Jefferson, who
had been chosen to write the initial draft, came up with its
memorable second sentence: 'We hold these truths to be
self-evident, that all men are created equal, that they are
endowed by their Creator with certain unalienable Rights, that
among these are Life, Liberty and the pursuit of Happiness.'

So, in a way, this historical document could be described as a Declaration of Rights!

Today we see people's rights strongly asserted within this world in many different ways. For example, there are employment rights, women's rights, civil rights, educational rights, and children's rights – to name but a few. Furthermore, in 1948 the United Nation's Declaration of Human Rights was issued and is currently being adopted country by country across this world. Of course, because all men and women have been created in God's image, rights are truly important. Therefore, as Christians, we should genuinely seek to uphold the rights of others.

'Because everyone is created in God's image, rights are important.'

1 Corinthians 9 is about rights. Now, contrary to what some may think, this chapter is not a digression by Paul from the issue of food sacrificed to idols, which he then picks up once more within the next chapter; rather, Paul is continuing and developing his argument about priorities in life, for Paul, after appealing to the strong for them to give up what they're entitled to for the sake of the weak, goes on to show that this is not some sort of abstract command which he's placing upon the Corinthian Christians. Why do I say that? Because Paul himself has had to do precisely this, to give up what was his by right for the sake of the gospel and others.

So what are Paul's rights, particularly as an apostle and

preacher of the gospel? In 1 Corinthians 9:1–14 we discover that Paul can expect the Christians and churches he's working on behalf of to provide for his needs and to support him financially. In other words, Paul's gospel proclamation is full-time, paid work. So it wouldn't be wrong for Paul to ask the Corinthian church to uphold his rights by providing for him and supporting him. In fact, within the Roman culture and society of that day, this was not only expected, it was also considered an affront for such a 'gift of support' to be rejected.[7] Therefore, the 'right thing' for Paul to do would be to accept and receive the support of the church. However, he doesn't, does he? 1 Corinthians 9:15: 'But I have not used any of these rights.' So why is that? Is it because it would be wrong to do so? Is it because it's a way to discredit others? No, it's for the sake of the gospel, as he explains in 1 Corinthians 9:12: 'If others have this right of support from you, shouldn't we have it all the more? But we did not use this right. On the contrary, we put up with everything rather than hinder the gospel of Christ.' Paul, despite any affront it may cause, decides not to receive financial support from the Corinthian church so that the impact of his own gospel preaching is not impeded.

At this point an interesting question arises: how does financial support from the Corinthian believers actually hinder the gospel? Or, to put it another way, how is the gospel furthered by Paul not asserting his rights? The answer is in two ways. First, Paul knows that financial support would, in reality, come from only one of the many factions existing within the Corinthian church at that time. Therefore, as this particular faction would effectively pay his wages, Paul would then be expected to toe its party line and, in being held hostage in this way, would hinder his proclamation of the gospel. Second, Paul wants to give voluntarily to the church for the sake of the gospel and this is the way he does it. Preaching for Paul is not voluntary, but a compulsion. 1 Corinthians 9:16: 'Woe to me if I do not preach.' However, he can give voluntarily to the church by preaching free of charge. 1 Corinthians 9:18: 'What then is my reward? Just this: that in preaching the gospel I may offer it free of charge, and so not make full use of my rights as a preacher of the gospel.' However, the bottom line is that Paul is far more interested in the gospel than his own rights.

In his book *The Screwtape Letters*, C. S. Lewis speaks of the allurement of the possessive pronoun 'my', as in 'my boots', 'my wife', 'my country'.[8] In other words, the mindset of this world is that I am at the centre of the universe. What matters is me. What's important is what I have. To put it another way, we're self-preoccupied and self-centred. As a consequence, it's 'my house' to be used as I want it to be used, not 'God's house' to be used as he wants it to be used; it's 'my car' to be used as I want it to be used, not 'God's car' to be used as he wants it to be used; it's 'my money' to be used as I want it to be used, not 'God's money' to be used as he wants it to be used. However, the truth is, everything that we receive is a gift from God and we're simply stewards who look after these things until we pass the baton on to those who follow. In particular, we're to use all that we have for the sake of God and his gospel. Indeed, this is the main teaching point of Jesus' parable of the shrewd manager. In Luke 16:9 Jesus says: 'I tell you, use worldly wealth to gain friends for yourselves, so that when it is gone, you will be welcomed into eternal dwellings.'

Now it's this worldly mindset, this self-preoccupation and self-centredness, which has invaded the hearts of the Corinthian Christians, for they are focussed upon their own rights. However, the good news of Jesus Christ is far more important than those rights. So Paul writes in 1 Corinthians 9:19–23: 'Though I am free and belong to no one, I have made myself a slave to everyone, to win as many as possible. To the Jews I became like a Jew, to win the Jews. To those under the law

'The Lord Jesus is more important than our rights.'

I became like one under the law … so as to win those under the law. To those not having the law I became like one not having the law … so as to win those not having the law. To the weak I became weak, to win the weak. I have become all things to all people so that by all possible means I might save some. I do all this for the sake of the gospel, that I may share in its blessings.' In effect, Paul gives up his rights, even to the point of making himself a slave to others, for the sake of the gospel.

In Philippians 1:12–18 we discover the same truth: Paul's priority is the gospel and as such it's more important than his own rights. Philippians 1:12: 'Now I want you to know, brothers and sisters, that what has happened to me has actually served to advance the gospel.' In other words, the proclamation of the good news of Jesus Christ is Paul's all-consuming passion. Indeed, when we read through this entire letter to the Philippian church, it's striking that Paul tells us very little about his own situation, even though he's in prison in Rome awaiting trial for his life! Yes, the occasional hint is dropped, a little piece of information here and there, but no more than that. Paul is almost careless concerning his own life and situation, for what matters to Paul is not how he is doing, but that the gospel is advancing.

As a result, with the gospel being preached among the palace guard and the Christians in Rome being strengthened through Paul's imprisonment to proclaim the gospel for themselves, Paul is confident to rest in God's hands concerning his own life and situation. In fact, even some preaching out of rivalry and envy against Paul doesn't faze him! Philippians 1:18: 'But what does it matter? The important thing is that in every way, whether from false motives or true, Christ is preached. And because of this, I rejoice.'

Again putting this all together, the third principle (or the second pillar) is this: the gospel takes precedence over my rights. It specifically relates to our relationship with those who are not Christians. Therefore, this time the question we should ask ourselves, before we make any important decisions, is: does what I plan to do make it easier for others to hear the gospel? Sometimes the answer to that question will lead to costly decisions for the sake of seeking to win the lost. However, we often really do need to abandon our own rights out of love for the lost – whoever they may be! This principle can also be described as the priority of the gospel's advance. In Acts 1:8 Jesus tells his disciples: '... you will be my witnesses in Jerusalem, and in all Judea and Samaria, and to the ends of the earth.'

The third pillar:
my spiritual well-being takes
precedence over my freedom

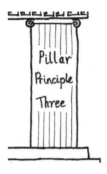

A young man moved to a new area of the country and began attending a new church. After a few weeks he came up to one of the church's pastors and complained, 'I don't like the worship of this church. I can't understand the preaching in this church. I don't find this church very friendly. I wasn't asked home for Sunday lunch in this church. I'm thinking of leaving this church.' Much to the young man's surprise, the pastor replied, 'It's not about you, stupid,' and walked away. Of course, there's much truth in the response of that pastor, though perhaps it was a little abrupt. Indeed, the truth of what he says reflects our first two pillars: an overriding concern for the church and the gospel.

However, there is also a sense in which we do actually need to be concerned about ourselves, for we need to watch carefully our own spiritual well-being and health, and this is the principle which Paul uses within 1 Corinthians 10 as he concludes his discussion on food sacrificed to idols. Furthermore, Paul explains this principle by bringing in two illustrations: one from history and the other from the Lord's Supper.

Let's begin with Paul's illustration from history which is found in 1 Corinthians 10:1–13. Paul takes us back to Mount Sinai, specifically to Exodus 32 and the story of the golden calf. The nation of Israel has been brought out of slavery within Egypt and, while their leader Moses is up on the mountain receiving the law and the covenant from God, the people begin to go astray; they cast an idol in the shape of a golden calf. Then in Exodus 32:6 we read: 'So the next day the people rose early and sacrificed burnt offerings and presented fellowship offerings. Afterwards they sat down to eat and drink and got up to indulge in revelry.' It's the second half of this verse which Paul quotes in 1 Corinthians 10:7.

So what's Paul's point with this illustration from history? Simply, to compare the Corinthian Christians with the Israelites at Mount Sinai. In other words, these Corinthians, like the Israelites, were also dangerously complacent, for they'd been baptised and were regularly partaking of the Lord's Supper. As a result, they thought that they were safe from any danger caused by eating meals within pagan temples. Yes, they rightly understood that pagan idols were nothing and that they were therefore free to participate in such meals. However, they failed to grasp the real, underlying danger that such participation may actually drag them back into their former lifestyle of idolatry. So Paul uses this illustration to make the Corinthians wake up to their danger.

Indeed, the similarity between the Corinthians and the people of Israel is striking. The people of Israel had also been baptised when they passed through the Red Sea (1 Corinthians 10:2). They also had spiritual food and spiritual drink: manna from heaven and water from the rock (1 Corinthians 10:3–4). And so they were also complacent, wrongly relying on those things. Of course, the most telling similarity is their feasting (1 Corinthians 10:7), for how like the Israelites the Corinthian Christians may have been when they too feasted within pagan temples. Therefore, Paul uses this illustration to warn the Corinthians. 1 Corinthians 10:11: 'These things happened to them as examples and were written down as warnings for us.' He's telling them to be very careful. 1 Corinthians 10:12: 'So, if you think you are standing firm, be careful that you don't fall!' In other words, don't use your freedom, which you have as a believer in Jesus Christ, to carelessly place yourself within a dangerous situation which may compromise and damage your own walk before God, for you're not as strong as you think you are.

The second illustration is from the Lord's Supper which is found in 1 Corinthians 10:14–22. In this illustration, Paul reminds the Corinthians that the Lord's Supper is not just a remembering, but that it's also a participating, for not only do we look upon the bread and wine, we also eat the bread and drink the wine. Now participating means that we commune with Jesus Christ. We fellowship with him. The baptist preacher, Charles Spurgeon, puts it like this: 'We not only eat of his bread but symbolically we feast upon him.'[9] Therefore, Paul writes, just as you participate in Jesus Christ in the Lord's Supper, so also you participate with demons when you feast within pagan temples. Yes, it's true that an idol is nothing as there's only one God (1 Corinthians 8:4) so that eating food sacrificed to idols is harmless in and of itself; nevertheless, behind all those idols are demons and as a Christian you must not be drawn into fellowship with them. He continues to explain in 1 Corinthians 10:20–22:

'Yes, we have freedom, but is that freedom beneficial to our spiritual health?'

'No, but the sacrifices of pagans are offered to demons, not to God, and I do not want you to be participants with demons. You cannot drink the cup of the Lord and the cup of demons too; you cannot have a part in both the Lord's table and the table of demons. Are we trying to arouse the Lord's jealousy? Are we stronger than he?'

Of course, the application for us today is that though we

may not be drawn to worship an idol of wood, metal, or stone, yet we may be drawn to worship possessions, ourselves, or pleasure. In other words, the danger is we can spend so much of our time, effort, and money on these things that they can become first within our hearts and draw us away from Jesus Christ. Yes, we may be free to do this or that, but doing this or that may not actually be beneficial for our own spiritual health, which is why Paul tells us in 1 Corinthians 10:14 to 'flee from idolatry'. Again, you're not as strong as you think you are.

Putting this all together, the fourth principle (or the third pillar) is this: my spiritual well-being takes precedence over my freedom. It specifically relates to our relationship with ourselves. So this time the question we should ask ourselves, before we make any important decisions, is: does what I plan to do benefit my own spiritual life or does it draw me away from Jesus Christ? Yes, I may be truly free to do something, but it may not be truly wise for me to do it. This principle can also be described as the priority of personal holiness. 1 John 3:2–3: 'But we know that when Christ appears, we shall be like him, for we shall see him as he is. All who have this hope in him purify themselves, just as he is pure.'

The overarching principle:
God's glory

So far we have discovered four principles: do what is right; do what is loving; do what promotes the gospel; and do what promotes my own growth in holiness. The fifth principle is the capstone. It's the overarching principle which provides the ultimate motivation for all that we do. What is it? It's that we're to do everything for the glory of God. 1 Corinthians 10:31: 'So whether you eat or drink or whatever you do, do it all for the glory of God.' Indeed, we're to persevere in this, for though we're finite, fallen, and lacking in strength, yet the God we serve is infinite, perfect, and all-powerful. Even more, he will help us, if we only look to him, and he is altogether worthy of our adoration and praise.

The Polish composer-pianist Paderewski was once scheduled to perform at a great American concert hall for a high-society extravaganza. In the audience was a mother with her fidgety nine-year-old son. Weary of waiting, the boy slipped away from her side, strangely drawn to the Steinway on the stage. Without initially being noticed by the audience, he sat down at the stool and began playing 'Chopsticks'. The roar of the crowd turned to shouts as hundreds yelled, 'Get that boy away from there!' However, when Paderewski heard the uproar backstage, he grabbed his coat and rushed over behind the boy. Reaching around him from behind, the master began to improvise a counter-melody. As the two of them played together, Paderewski kept whispering in the boy's ear, 'Keep going. Don't quit, son. Don't stop. Don't stop.' And that's like God with us, for though we seek to do what's best for him, his gospel, and his church, yet what we do is only ever like playing 'Chopsticks' on the Steinway. However, God is behind us. God is playing a beautiful counter-melody. God is working out through our feeble efforts all his glorious purposes of grace. And surely that should motivate us to do what's right and best. Though certainly weak and sinful, yet we're to persevere in doing everything for his glory.

In Philippians 1:19–21, this priority of God's glory is vividly portrayed to us in the attitude of Paul while he's languishing in prison in Rome awaiting trial for his life. Consider Philippians

1:19: 'I know that through your prayers and God's provision of the Spirit of Jesus Christ what has happened to me will turn out for my deliverance.' So what deliverance is Paul seeking? Is it release from his imprisonment and escape from the threat of imminent death which is hanging over him? In fact, wouldn't this be exactly what the Christians in Philippi were praying for? But no, for consider now Philippians 1:20–21: 'I eagerly expect and hope that I will in no way be ashamed, but will have sufficient courage so that now as always Christ will be exalted in my body, whether by life or by death. For to me, to live is Christ and to die is gain.'

In other words, Paul is not so much concerned about his appearance before the imperial court of Rome, but about his appearance before the court of God. Will he be vindicated then? Indeed, perhaps Paul had in mind the words of Jesus in Mark 8:38: 'If anyone is ashamed of me and my words in this adulterous and sinful generation, the Son of Man will be ashamed of them when he comes in his Father's glory with the holy angels.' So Paul's desire is to remain faithful to Jesus Christ in the midst of the trial he faces before Caesar. Will Jesus be ashamed of Paul or will Jesus be exalted by Paul's words and actions during the cross examination, the verdict, and the possible execution? Which will it be? For Paul is not interested in survival or being

> 'Paul's desire is to remain faithful to God in the midst of trials.'

delivered from the court of man; rather, he's only interested in standing firm and being faithful to his adored Saviour and Lord so that Jesus Christ would not be dishonoured through him. Paul's priority is the glory of Jesus Christ.

In one of her books, Elisabeth Elliott, an American missionary, speaks of two adventurers who stopped by to see her.[10] They were loaded down with equipment ready for the rainforest east of the Andes and had come seeking advice from her. Perhaps they were looking for a few phrases to help them converse with the native South Americans. Elisabeth Elliott writes: 'Sometimes we come to God as the two adventurers came to me – confident and, we think, well-informed and well equipped. But has it occurred to us that with all our accumulation of stuff, something is missing?' She goes on to suggest that we often ask God for too little: a yes or no answer to a simple question; perhaps a road sign, something quick and easy to point the way. She continues: 'What we really ought to have is the Guide himself. Maps, road signs, a few useful phrases are things, but infinitely better is someone who has been there before and knows the way.' In other words, we need God himself, to walk with him, to persevere in his strength not ours, and to live for his glory. Therefore, as we walk through life and in all our decisions and plans, we need God's presence with us and his glory always before us. And if we do that, we can then face all the difficulties and decisions of life with genuine confidence. As Romans 8:31–32 so helpfully explains: 'What, then, can we say in response to these things? If God is for us, who can be against us? He who did not spare his own Son, but gave him up for us all – how will he not also, along with him, graciously give us all things?'

To summarise: the overarching principle is: we're to do what we do, ultimately and always, for the glory of God. It specifically relates to our relationship with God. This principle can also be described as the priority of exalting Jesus Christ. Colossians 1:18: 'And he [the Son] is the head of the body, the church; he is the beginning and the firstborn from among the dead, so that in everything he might have the supremacy.'

Case studies

So far we've considered only the theory: what the Bible teaches on how we're to make wise decisions. We've discovered five principles.[11]

1. We're always to do what is right and never to do what is wrong
2. Love takes precedence over knowledge
3. The gospel takes precedence over my rights
4. My spiritual well-being takes precedence over my freedom
5. We're to do what we do, always and ultimately, for God's glory

In other words, we're to do what's right, the first principle, to do what's important, the next three principles, and to do what's best, the final principle. Alternatively, these five principles can be expressed as one constraint and four priorities.

1. The constraint of God's moral law
2. The priority of the local church's spiritual growth and well-being
3. The priority of the gospel's advance
4. The priority of personal holiness
5. The priority of exalting Jesus Christ

Let's seek now to use these five principles within the messy complications of everyday life. We shall do this by considering five short case studies. Ideally, these case studies should be discussed within small groups. In addition, extra teaching from the Bible is given relating to these five different areas of life.

Case study 1: guidance for work

John and Jo are a recently-married couple in the church. They are young-in-faith Christians who are expecting their first child in a few months time. John has been offered a much better paid job elsewhere in the country. By using the five principles on guidance and also referring to Ephesians 5:25; Colossians 3:23–24; Hebrews 10:24–25; 1 Peter 3:7 what different aspects of their life do John and Jo need to consider before John accepts or declines this new job?

In Ephesians 6:5–9 and Colossians 3:22–4:1 we're given instruction by Paul which is applicable to both employees and employers. Employees are to obey and respect their employers, not mindlessly, begrudgingly, or with craven fear, but wholeheartedly and with sincerity. Even more, our work is to be done as to the Lord. Therefore, it matters not so much what our employers think or do, but what God thinks and does. Ephesians 6:7–8: 'Serve wholeheartedly, as if you were serving the Lord, not people, because you know that the Lord will reward each one for whatever good they do, whether they are slave or free.' Employers are to treat all people with dignity because all people are made in God's image. What is important is not a job done well with people walked over, but a job done not so well with people respected, for people matter to God.

Case study 2: guidance for the church

Leah and Jane have been close friends for many years. They are both Christians and members of the same local church. However, Jane has little time for two or three of the teenage girls connected to the church who are from poorer families and not Christians. By using the five principles on guidance and also referring to Romans 15:1–7; Galatians 6:10; Ephesians 4:3; Philippians 2:1–11 what should Leah do?

In Acts 2:42–47 we have a description of church life. The local church is a living, loving body and community of people who're committed to each other and to Jesus Christ so that together they may worship and serve God. In particular, all Christians should be part of a local church: identified with it, committed to it, and loving the members of it. The local church provides nurture, love, and care. Galatians 6:2: 'Carry each other's burdens, and in this way you will fulfil the law of Christ.' The local church equips and matures. Ephesians 4:11–13: 'So Christ himself gave the apostles, the prophets, the evangelists, the pastors and teachers, to equip his people for works of service, so that the body of Christ may be built up until we all reach unity in the faith and in the knowledge of the Son of God and become mature, attaining to the whole measure of the fullness of Christ.' The local church provides fellowship, which in itself is a witness to those outside the church. Acts 2:46–47: 'Every day they continued to meet together with glad and sincere hearts, praising God and enjoying the favour of all the people. And the Lord added to their number daily those who were being saved.' The local church gives opportunity for worship together and to receive teaching from God's word. Psalm 100:2: 'Worship the LORD with gladness; come before him with joyful songs.' 2 Timothy 3:16–17: 'All Scripture is God-breathed and useful for teaching, rebuking, correcting and training in righteousness, so that the servant of God may be thoroughly equipped for every good work.'

Case study 3: guidance for family

When Ben was young, his mother went out, leaving him in charge of his younger sister Sally. In his mother's absence, Ben discovered some bottles of coloured ink and decided to paint his sister's portrait. He made an appalling mess! By using the five principles on guidance and also referring to Ephesians 6:4 and Colossians 3:21 what should his mother's reaction be when she came home?

To complete the story, when his mother came back, she said nothing about the terrible ink stains. Instead, she picked up the piece of paper on which he'd been working and exclaimed, 'Why, it's Sally!' Then she stooped and kissed him. That Ben was Benjamin West, who went on to become a distinguished artist. Benjamin West often used to say, 'My mother's kiss made me a painter!' I'm not excusing the mess and I'm sure Ben's mother didn't either, but if she'd only come down on him like a ton of bricks and ignored his efforts at painting, I think he would've been rightly resentful.

In Ephesians 6:1–4 and Colossians 3:20–21 we're given by Paul instruction on family life. Interestingly, children are addressed directly by Paul within the church. It seems that Paul expects the children within the church to hear this letter read to them. In other words, Paul treated children with dignity and respect. He also expected them to understand what he had written. As parents stand in God's place in their relationship to their children, so children are to obey their parents. They're also to honour them: to look up to them and be committed to their well-being. So what should a child do if a parent doesn't live in such a way that demands corresponding obedience and honour, for example an alcoholic father or a worldly mother? They're still to honour and obey them, unless that obedience explicitly contradicts the revealed moral law of God. Fathers are responsible for ensuring that children receive instruction and discipline. Both are required, for two things can exasperate a child: discipline when the child doesn't know why and a lecture with no corresponding discipline to show why it needs to be heard and obeyed.

Case study 4: guidance for marriage

Mary is married to Mark. He's a good husband. He works hard. He loves her. He provides for her in many ways. However, he seems to shirk responsibility. He doesn't take the lead in many of the decisions that have to be made. By using the five principles on guidance and also referring to Ephesians 5:22–33, what should both Mark and Mary do?

Ephesians 5:22–33; Colossians 3:18–19; 1 Peter 3:1–7 give detailed instruction on how husbands and wives are to relate to one another within a marriage. Marriage is a public, lifelong, exclusive, and intimate covenant between one man and one woman in the sight of God. Husbands are to be loving heads of their families. They're to love their wives as Jesus Christ loved the church. Therefore, it's love to the uttermost. It's a focussed, faithful, self-denying love. They're also to be servant leaders, taking responsibility in order to protect and provide for their wives so that their wives may reflect something of the beauty of Jesus Christ. Wives are to be willingly submissive. A submissive wife will not threaten, but encourage her husband's leadership. She gives all the wise input she can so that her husband can think things through from her perspective as well as his own. Submission is not because of inferiority, but to the Lord. It's not weakness, but meekness. It may even require a wife, for her husband's benefit, to stand against him when he's wrong.

Case study 5: guidance for pre-marital relationships

Archie is a recently-converted teenager from a non-Christian family. Anna goes to the same church as Archie. Her parents are members of the church. However, though Anna is favourably disposed towards the Christian faith, she has not made any profession of faith. Archie and Anna get along well within the youth group. By using the five principles on guidance and also referring to 1 Corinthians 7:32–35 and 2 Corinthians 6:14–15, should Archie develop the relationship more?

Simon and Sue are a Christian couple soon to be married. In their relationship Simon wants them to spend most of their time together alone and not with other Christian friends. By using the five principles on guidance and also referring to Proverbs 27:10, 28:26; Galatians 6:1–2; Philippians 2:3–4 in what ways can this be damaging to their relationship?

Proverbs 7 and 1 Thessalonians 4:3–8 warn against illicit relationships outside of marriage. Two principles can be drawn relating specifically to pre-marital relationships. First, do not pursue a relationship simply for the sake of romance, a good time, or gaining experience; rather, only enter into a relationship if long-term commitment is the goal. Proverbs 3:3: 'Let love and faithfulness never leave you; bind them round your neck, write them on the tablet of your heart.' Second, in any pre-marital relationship both parties are responsible for guarding the purity of body and heart. Romance must be controlled by wisdom. Proverbs 2:11: 'Discretion will protect you, and understanding will guard you.'

Further reading

- *Decision Making and the Will of God: A Biblical Alternative to the Traditional View*, Garry Friesen with J. Robin Maxson (Multnomah, 1980)

- *Just Do Something: A Liberating Approach to Finding God's Will*, Kevin DeYoung (Moody Press, 2014)

- *True Spirituality*, Vaughan Roberts (IVP, 2011)

Notes

1. *True Spirituality*, Vaughan Roberts (IVP, 2011), pages 105–133. I'm indebted to Vaughan Roberts for much that is within this book.
2. I'm indebted to Brian Edwards in his book *How Do We Get Guidance?* (DayOne, 1992) for these six incorrect ways for guidance.
3. *Your Father Loves You*, James Packer (Harold Shaw Publishers, 1986), page for 13 October.
4. *A Call to Spiritual Reformation*, D. A. Carson (IVP, 1992), pages 102–103.
5. *Decision Making and the Will of God: A Biblical Alternative to the Traditional View*, Garry Friesen with J. Robin Maxson (Multnomah, 1980), page 187.
6. Ibid., pages 177–179.

7. *1 Corinthians: A Shorter Exegetical and Pastoral Commentary*, Anthony C. Thistelton (Eerdmans, 2006), page 140.
8. *The Screwtape Letters*, C. S. Lewis (Harper Collins, 2002), letter 21.
9. *Metropolitan Tabernacle Pulpit Volume 38*, Charles Haddon Spurgeon (The Banner of Truth, 1987), sermon 2268.
10. *A Slow and Certain Light: Thoughts on the guidance of God*, Elisabeth Elliott (Abingdon Press, 1982).
11. See *True Spirituality*, Vaughan Roberts (IVP, 2011), page 133 for a diagram which helpfully describes these principles as a flowchart.